THE FOUR DIMENSIONS OF THE MINISTRY OF CHRIST

Richard D. Harvey

Rickie,

Thanks for paving the way and for tremendous encouragement to complete this

God Bless!

<u>Dedication</u>

This book is dedicated to the women in my life who have served as the foundation for my desire to be all that God wants me to be so that I can be all that I can be for them. To my wife, Kim, I can't seem to find any short poem, verse or phrase that will do justice to the whole of what you have meant to me. You have been the personification of the term "helpmate," and all my significant achievements to date have been inspired and facilitated by your support. To my daughters, Alex, Krystani, Jessica, and Zahra, this very book was truly inspired by you. You are my arrows and the teaching in this book is my "bow." To my mother, Tommie, you were my first teacher and example. You infected me with a love for God and a love for the people that God loves.

Acknowledgements

I wish to acknowledge a host of people who have either directly (via proofreading) or indirectly (via influencing me) contributed to this book. First of all, I want to thank Kim Harvey for proofreading the earlier, and sincerely "rougher drafts." I would also like to thank Paul Hellickson, Rodney Straughter, and Kim Tolliver for their extremely helpful edits and suggestions on this manuscript.

I would like to thank Pastors Harold Coleman, Bill Bray, Daniel Nicholson, and BCM director Charles Lillard for the wisdom that you have imparted and the profound examples that you have been of Godly character. I want to especially thank Pastor Anthony Coleman and Pastor Ted Boldin. You have both directly impacted the development of my character and faith, and created opportunities for my giftings to be nurtured and flourish. Finally, I want to give a very special thanks to Bishop Raphael Green. I regret that my vocabulary does not yet possess the complexity to appropriately describe the profundity of your influence on me. Let me simply say, that because of you "Daddy's dream" has become my dream and obsession. Your teachings have molded my understanding and passion for the vision, call, and strategies of God.

Preface

The overall purpose of this book is to develop discipleship among people at various levels in their Christian walk. For the person who has been recently born again, this book might serve as a simple orientation to "what it's all about". For the person who has been walking with Jesus for some time, this book might help them to clarify and see the Bible and ministry of Jesus Christ from a different perspective.

In order to "understand" anything we have to be able to relate it to something else or be able to place it in a category (this is called *conceptualizing*). For example, we might best be able to understand what an *Alfa Romeo* is by first understanding that it is a type of car. Knowing that an Alfa Romeo relates to or belongs in the category of "car" drastically increases our ability to understand it. Perhaps you have never seen one before, but I bet you can guess a lot about it (i.e., what it does, what its parts are, etc.) just from knowing that it is a type of car.

Many find the Bible difficult and even boring to read because they frankly don't understand it. For the most part, they don't understand it because they can't (here's that big word again!) *conceptualize* it. There are nevertheless plenty of conceptual categories in the Bible. For example, you could think of the Bible as being divided up into two main categories: Old Testament / New Testament. On the other hand, you could think of the 66 books of the Bible as being divided up into topical categories: Law / History / Poetry /Prophecy / Gospels / Doctrine / Pastoral. However, these are either too broad or are focused more around the Bible as a piece of literature rather than as a tool for understanding God's message to the church. As a result, they don't really help people solve the problem of understanding the Bible or more importantly God's will for their life.

Hence, a more specific goal of this book is to provide a conceptual tool that will help us all to better understand how to think about the Bible. However, this book is not meant to merely serve as a bible study tool. While the strategy is to better acquaint the reader with the word of God, the objective is to better acquaint them with the *God of the word*. It is important to remember that we should study the Bible, not just for the "info," but rather so that we might understand the will of God and live our lives to please Him and reflect His glory in the earth. Thus, this book, in helping us to understand the Bible, has the ultimate goal of helping us to understand the will of God for our lives. The will of God contains His goals, strategies, and guidelines for how to live our lives. As we learn these, we will also learn how to more fully cooperate with His will in our day and time.

Table of Contents

Chapter 1

Introduction

A few weeks ago, I heard the now late Dr. D. James Kennedy say on television that the Bible could be divided into three themes: *generation, degeneration*, and *regeneration*. He also pointed out the ironic fact that both generation (i.e., creation) and degeneration (i.e., fall) occur within the first three chapters of the Bible. Thus, the rest of the Bible is all about the third theme, regeneration. I found this simple categorization tool quite interesting. Of course, the regeneration theme covers a lot of leftover ground (i.e., the remainder of the book of Genesis and the other 65 books of the Bible). We Christians know that *regeneration* is the sole responsibility of our Lord Jesus Christ. Thus, the third theme of regeneration is really all about the plan, the accomplishment, and the abiding effects of the work of Jesus Christ.

The main point of this book is to suggest that we could both effectively and efficiently categorize all of what the Bible has to say about this regenerative ministry of Jesus Christ into four categories: FOR US, IN US, THROUGH US, and TO US. More specifically:

1) What Christ has already done **FOR US.** The foundation of the Old Testament, the sacrifice and then resurrection of Christ for our sins all reflect what God has already done FOR US.
2) What Christ is now doing **IN US.** The current development of our faith and God-like character (i.e., discipleship) all

reflect the work that God is currently attempting to do within His body, that is, IN US.

3) What Christ desires and is attempting to do **THROUGH US.** The calling upon the church to be ambassadors and vessels, through which God will reconcile the world to Himself, reflects the ministry of Christ THROUGH US.

4) What Christ will ultimately do **TO US.** This dimension reflects our ultimate destiny. The coming glorification and Sabbath-rest for the people of God at the end of times indicate what God will ultimately do TO US. The process that God began FOR US, and is now working both IN US and THROUGH US will be consummated when God gives the completion of His glory and rest TO US (i.e., "the summing up of all things in Christ"- Eph. 1:10).

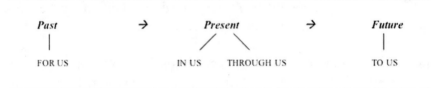

Figure 1.1 *Dimensions of Time and Ministry of Christ.*

These four dimensions rest along three time periods of Christ's ministry: Past, Present and Future (See Figure 1.1). What God has done FOR US reflects the Past. Thus, this work has been finished. What God is attempting to do both IN US and THROUGH US are a part of the Present ministry of Christ. These two dimensions reflect God's current work of growing and maturing His church. Finally, what God is going to do TO US reflects the future completed perfection of His church.

Each of these four dimensions requires a response on the part of the believer once they are understood and embraced (see Table 1.1). Because what Christ has done FOR US has already been completed, the required response to this dimension is *acceptance.* That is, we must accept the completed work of Christ provided for us and not waste our time attempting to achieve what we have already received (please note the rhyme!). In order for God to achieve what He is attempting to do IN US, we must respond to His work with *submission*. God is a gentle God and does not force His desires upon us. Thus, we must submit and be obedient to His will in order for true change to take place in us. Our response to what God is attempting to do THROUGH US must be *cooperation*. That is, we must learn how to cooperate or work with the flow of the Holy Spirit through us. Finally, we must respond to God's picture of what He plans to do TO US with sincere *expectation*. This expectation of God's pre-determined destiny (also known as *Hope!*) is the basis of faith, which in turn, is the key ingredient for everything else that we do.

Table 1.1 **Responses of the Believer to each dimension**

FOR US: *Acceptance*	**IN US:** *Submission*
TO US: *Expectation*	**THROUGH US:** *Cooperation*

Not only is it important to understand these four dimensions of the ministry of Christ individually, but also it is important to understand how they are related to each other. For example, we can't truly understand the depth of what God is trying to do IN US or THROUGH US without first understanding what He has done FOR US. What He has done FOR US is the foundation for what He is attempting to do both IN US and THROUGH US. In a sense, what He is doing IN US and THROUGH US is really only a continuation of what He already began FOR US. That's why the Bible says that He who begun a good work in you will continue it until completion (Phil. 1:6). Also, God can only do THROUGH US what He has first done IN US. Think about it, you simply can't pour water out of a glass until you have first poured water into the glass. The examples could go on and on. However, the main point is that we need each of these dimensions to help balance our understanding of the others. (see Figure 1.2)

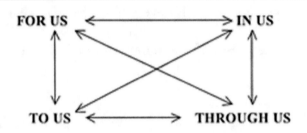

Figure 1.2 *Interdependence of the four dimensions*

The next four chapters in this book deal with each of these dimensions and our responses to them in greater detail. The structure of each chapter is similar. The first part of each chapter discusses important biblical topics that fit within that particular dimension. As you will see, the topics that are discussed cover a wide variety of other topics that might be placed within that dimension as well. If this book is being used as either a personal or group Bible study aid, the reader might spend some time considering how other important topics are related to each of the main topics in the chapters.

The last part of each chapter is devoted to considering why the information in the chapter is important to know and what the reader should do with the information. This is the practical application part of the chapter. *Knowledge* (i.e., information) is only useful when it is transformed into *wisdom* (i.e., the ability to apply knowledge). Thus, practical instructions on how to respond to the insights of the chapters will also be presented. For this reason, each chapter could be used as a personal or group devotional as well.

Hopefully, the reader will find each chapter to be useful for both better understanding the Bible and as a devotional guide. Let the journey begin...

Chapter 2

For Us

Understanding what God has done FOR US is the backbone of Christianity. It is the foundation on which the other three dimensions sit. To talk about what God has done for us is essentially to talk about the Gospel of His Grace.

God's grace means the *gift* of His favor. In the New Testament, *grace* is compared and contrasted to the *law* of the Old Testament. The point of this comparison is to distinguish the "gift" of God's favor from the "deeds" required to earn it. The Law of the Old Testament required people to do righteous acts or deeds in order to earn favor with God and thus have blessings (see Deuteronomy 28). In contrast to the Law of the Old Testament, the point of the Gospel of Grace is that it is impossible to earn God's favor through doing righteous deeds; however, through Christ, God's favor is given as a gift to all who will accept it.

Our tendency to abbreviate the "Gospel" has unfortunately led to widespread ignorance about the role of *Grace* in that Gospel. I often like to caution people not to treat the teaching of Grace as just another doctrine. It is, in fact, THE doctrine that is the foundation for all others. Grace is not just some aspect **of the** Gospel; Grace **is the** Gospel of Jesus Christ!

To understand what God has done FOR US is to understand the complete Gospel of His Grace. There are three essential aspects to this Gospel: 1) Sacrifice, 2) Justification, and 3) Elevation (as illustrated in Figure 2.1).

Jesus' Sacrifice $\longrightarrow$ Justification $\longrightarrow$ Our Elevation

Figure 2.1 *Three essentials of the Gospel*

Sacrifice

In the Old Testament, God's people, the Israelites, were required to make animal sacrifices as payment for the debt of sin. The truth is, however, this was only done for the sake of their conscience. In reality, these animal sacrifices were not able to actually remove their sins (Heb 10:1-4). In fact, the very purpose for these sacrifices was to serve as a reminder to them that they were helplessly sinful (Heb 10:3). So, their sacrifices were more of a symbolic gesture rather than a practical solution to their problem with sin.

The symbol was a vivid one. Imagine that one day you have the pleasure of watching a baby sheep being born. You watch that little sheep day after day nurse from its mother. You name that little sheep and play with it. It becomes dear to you. Then one day, you lead that little sheep to the tabernacle where a Priest basically butchers, dissects, and then burns it. That poor little innocent sheep! Imagine the horror of a young child who has to watch this.

The question now becomes, what could this sacrifice possibly be symbolic of? For one, it is symbolic of the horror of sin. The message is clear: sin brings death to the innocent! This message is particularly important when we ponder questions like "why is there so much suffering in the world." The answer eventually comes down to sin. However, there is a greater reality to this symbol and that is the reality of Christ's sacrifice on the cross. Jesus is unarguably the most innocent person who ever lived, seeing that he is the only person deemed to be without sin. And yet, He was butchered for the sins of the world. So, these innocent animal sacrifices were primarily symbolic of the sacrifice that Jesus would one day make FOR US.

Let's probe this a little deeper by flashing back again to the Old Testament. The Bible says that the Law of Moses was the standard used to judge and thus convict people of sin (Rom 7:7,8; Gal. 3:19-25). During its existence, this law was placed into a box called the Ark of the Covenant, which sat in the most secluded place in the tabernacle (i.e., the Holy of Holies). The lid on the Ark of the Covenant was basically a seat called the Mercy Seat (Ex. 25:21). In the original Hebrew, the word translated as *Mercy Seat* is "kap-po-reth", and means "to cover", in two ways: 1) as a noun, meaning a lid, or a top and 2) as a verb, meaning to pardon or atone for, as in to cover a debt. Get the point? Although there was a law in the Ark that was judging and convicting God's people of sin, God was covering that all up with His mercy. Just in case you didn't know: "mercy" is where you don't get the punishment that you deserve (in contrast "grace" is where you get the blessing that you don't deserve). So, the mercy seat was preventing the peoples' sin from being counted against them (see 2 Cor. 5:18).

We later learn that the Mercy Seat was in fact a symbolic representation of the atoning sacrifice that Christ made FOR US (Heb. 10). It seems as though this mercy seat operated as a type of credit card for sin. Every time they sinned, rather than having to immediately pay the price (i.e., which was death) it was simply charged to an account. Not only this, but also God in His foreknowledge charged all future sins to this credit card (i.e., a pre-pay). When Jesus died, He paid the balance in full and then canceled the card! [and everyone with a credit card balance said: Amen!]

The "Gospel" of what God has done FOR US really begins with understanding the sacrifice that Christ made on our behalf. As the completion of the sin offerings and burnt offerings in the Old Testament, God presented Jesus as the sacrifice to pay the price of sin (Rom 3:25; Heb. 10). Thus, the debt due for your sin has been paid off!

It is very difficult to make payments on an account that not only has a zero balance but has been canceled altogether. Some years ago, I was attempting to clear up an issue with a collection agency. They kept insisting that I owed a bill with a former vendor and wanted me to pay them the balance. However, I knew that I had paid off the bill before I canceled the account. Every time I called the vendor they said that they had no record of my account. After the bill was paid, the account was closed and basically erased from their records. Yet, I had a hard time trying to get that information from the vendor to the collection agency. I then suspected the collection agency of fraud and threatened to take action. I haven't heard from them since! The devil works like this collection agency, attempting to perpetuate a fraud by telling us that we owe God a balance in an attempt to get us to do something on our own to pay for it. But, when we contact God, there is no balance, no account, and no record! Jesus truly paid it all and canceled the account (Col. 2:14).

Justification

The second part of what God has done FOR US involves the concepts of "justification" and "righteousness." The Bible teaches that the sacrifice of Christ leads to the justification of those who accept Him (that is, put Him in charge of their lives). The term "justification" means to be legally declared "right" with God. Furthermore, to be *right* is to be in a satisfactory condition or status. Only when there is no balance or debt, are we in complete satisfactory status with the lender. Unfortunately, sin has put us in serious debt to God. However, when we apply the sacrifice of Christ to our lives by accepting Him, we are in effect applying His payment to our debt of sin. So, in effect, the sacrifice that Christ gave makes us legally "righteous." In sum, when we put Christ in charge of our life, your debt is paid, and you are declared "righteous" before God.

The main point about our righteousness is to make sure that it remains connected to the first step (i.e., Christ's Sacrifice). The temptation has always been to see our righteousness as a result of our own sacrifices rather than Jesus' sacrifice. Another temptation has been to see Christ's sacrifice as having only partially fulfilled our debt and that we must now complete it by doing good things and avoiding bad things. It is this first temptation that Paul attempted to deal with in the first 10 chapters of Romans and the first five chapters of Galatians (...and other places). People were confused and thinking that their righteousness (and hence their salvation) depended upon their good works rather than Christ's good work. It is the second temptation that Paul attempted to deal with when he wrote the book of Colossians. Heretical teachers were teaching people that although the sacrifice of Jesus was the beginning, they had to do some other stuff to get the fullness of the gospel. Paul's message is pointedly clear in this book: "...you have been given fullness in Christ..." (Col. 2:10). For either temptation, it is important that we understand that our righteousness is because of Christ's sacrifice and not because of anything we do. Our sacrifices of good deeds cannot settle the debt (Eph 2:8,9; Heb. 10:1-10).

The topics of Righteousness and Justification are the heart of the Gospel (Rom. 1:17). They preoccupy the majority of New Testament doctrine. The first 10 chapters of Romans and all but the last chapter of Galatians directly deal with the subject of *justification by grace through faith.* That is, they drive home the point that we get declared righteous in God's court only when we accept by faith (i.e., rely upon) the grace (i.e., a gift that is given, not worked for) of His sacrifice. However, most other doctrinal books of the Bible provide important nuggets on this topic as well (e.g., Eph 1:3-9, 2:8,9; Phil. 3:1-11; Col. 2:13-23, etc.). So, the second part of what God has done FOR US is to legally declare us righteous (i.e., justification) after we accept the sacrifice of Christ.

Elevation

The third aspect of what God has done FOR US flows from our justification. As a result of our having been declared righteous with God, God elevates our status with respect to both himself and the world. Think about it this way (to continue the credit card analogy earlier): with a clean debt slate and new credit score of 850, your status would be tremendously altered. People with those scores have levels of privilege not available to others. The principles they live by (e.g., interest charges) and the access they have (e.g., Platinum memberships, V.I.P, etc.) are different. They are not better than anyone else, but they are better off! They may not possess more than anyone, but when emergencies arise, they are in a much better position to use their credit to adapt and deal with them.

The most important aspect of our elevation is our conversion from sinners to sons and daughters of almighty God (Gal. 4:4-7). This conversion has a number of important implications. One of the most important is the implication that it has for our *identity*. Our identity is a part of our soul that is composed of the many beliefs that we have about ourselves. Our identities determine the way we will respond to certain objects and events. When we were sinners, we believed things about our selves that were sinful. Furthermore, we responded to objects and situations like sinners. Now that we have been elevated to the position of children of God, it is important that we see ourselves as such. We must now respond to objects and situations like sons and daughters of God. Unfortunately, the phrase "What would Jesus Do" became more faddish than transforming. Nevertheless, it is the right mentality to have.

Being a child of God has privileges of many kinds, just as any child would or should have with his or her father. Perhaps the greatest privilege that any child would have is access. Not only would the child have access to their father's reputation and resources, but more importantly, access to the father himself. Likewise, as children of God, we have access to God Himself, in fact, whenever we want, through prayer (and yes we are spoiled, and like most spoiled children, we take it for granted and neither appreciate nor use it). This access means that through our elevated status we have both peace and favor with God as well.

The Bible says that since we have received justification, we now have "peace" with God (Rom. 5:1). To have peace with anything typically means to have freedom from conflict. So, peace with God means freedom from conflict with God but more than that, it means to have unity with God. Also, the flipside of having peace with God, is having favor with God. The Bible says that we now exist in an abiding state of grace, which in this case means an abiding state of favor with God (Rom 5:2). To have "favor" with someone means that the other person has an attitude of "good will" toward you. Thus, to have favor with God is to know that God has good will toward you. It stands to reason that if God has good will toward you, then His will is good for you! So the second aspect of our newly elevated status is that we have obtained both peace and good will from God.

Thus, it was of little surprise that the first introduction of Jesus to the world by the angels began with "Glory to God in the highest, and on earth <u>peace, goodwill</u> toward men!" (Luke 2:14, NKJV).

With respect to how our newly elevated status relates to the rest of the world, God has elevated us to *heavenly realms*. Ephesians 2:6 reads "And God raised us up with Christ and seated us with Him in the heavenly realms in Christ Jesus." A "realm" is a particular area over which someone rules. It is clear that the *heavenly realm* would be the area where God rules. So, what does this all mean.... being elevated to heavenly realms? Well, it is clear that the answer is not physical (at least not yet!). We don't just rocket out of here immediately after we get saved. Unfortunately, it isn't mental either. We don't just automatically start having heavenly desires, feelings, and thoughts after we get saved either (go ahead and exhale!). It is, in fact, *spiritual*. Heavenly realms are *spiritual realms*. When we got saved, we became alive spiritually, which means that the core spiritual aspect of who we are began to exist in a realm where God rules. Furthermore, we now have the authority and opportunity to transfer that rule across the other realms in which we exist (i.e., mental, physical). More importantly, we can also choose which of those realms, and the rules therein, will have the ultimate rule in our lives. Will our lives ultimately be ruled and governed more by the physical, mental, or spiritual realm? { You might want to read this paragraph again because it got a little deep}

It is clear that by elevating us to the heavenly realm, God intends for us to be ruled by spiritual rules (of course, His!). There are a number of biblical verses that serve as premises to this conclusion. Consider the fact that although we are "in" the world, we are not "of" the world (John 17: 13-16). Also, the scriptures make it clear that we are dead to the basic principles of this world (Col 2:20). Furthermore, we are commanded to not love the world because the stuff that's in the world is really nothing more than lust, pride, and greed (1 John 2:15,16).

Now before you get totally freaked out about this elevation stuff, note that I am not trying to say that we are not subject to mental or natural laws. Go jump off a bridge and the physical law of gravity will quickly introduce you to the ground. Commit a crime and the civil law of police will introduce you to your future cellmate. It's not that we are not subject to mental and natural laws, it's that we are not subject to mental and natural laws ONLY or even PRIMARILY! We are also subject to spiritual laws and these spiritual laws are more dominant than mental and natural laws. We are under the primary governance of spiritual laws and when the mental and natural conflict with them, the spiritual overrule them. Occasionally, the choice is actually ours to make. The phrase "whose report will you believe" is actually a question of whether we are going to choose the spiritual as the dominant ruler in our circumstance, not necessarily a denial of the mental and natural. This is why healing and prosperity can override the normal prognosis of illness and lower socio-economic status in a Christian's life.

In sum, what God has done FOR US might be summed up in three aspects of the Gospel: 1) The ultimate sacrifice that Christ paid for sin, 2) the legal declaration of our righteousness, and 3) the elevation of our status to being children of God, having peace and favor with God, and existing with God under the primary governance of His spiritual laws.

Why do we need to know this and what do we do with this info?

Why do we need to know what God has done FOR US? There are at least two reasons. First of all, we need to know what God has done for us so that we don't try to achieve through our own efforts things that God has already provided. Many Christians waste too much of their time begging and pleading for what they already have (i.e., righteousness). They do good deeds, but not from the right perspective. This then leads to the illusion of self-righteousness, which produces either pride, in the case of when they actually experience success at doing good deeds, or condemnation in the case where they fail in their attempt to do good deeds. But neither pride nor condemnation are outcomes that come from God. So, knowing what God has already done FOR US, prevents us from working in vain to earn what has already been given to us.

The second reason why we need to know what God has done for us proceeds from the first. When we understand the foundation of Christianity, we don't regress back to what the Bible calls "dead works" (i.e., good deeds that are supposed to get you righteousness, but don't). Instead, we are now ready to press on and make progress. What God has done FOR US serves as the foundation for understanding the other three dimensions of what God is trying to do IN US and THROUGH US and ultimately, TO US. So, the second reason we need to know what God has done FOR US is so that we can better understand the distinctive roles of the other three dimensions of Christ's ministry.

What do you do with the information of what Christ has done FOR US? Well, the key word in responding to what Christ has done FOR US is <u>acceptance</u>. Remember that all of it is a "gift" (remember *grace*). And what do you do with a gift? You simply, *accept it!* So, you must simply recognize the fact that Christ provided the sacrifice for our sins, justification, and elevation. Then simply say, "I accept" to Christ for all that He has provided FOR US. You should do that right now! Just talk to Christ right now and confess and thank Him for each of the following:

1) His sacrifice for your sins,
2) your legal justification and declaration of righteous in the eyes of God,
3) the fact that you have peace and favor with God, and
4) declare His governance and rule over your life.

Chapter 3

In Us

God is trying to develop *Faith* and *Character* IN US. The biblical topics of Faith and Character are extremely important because many other biblical topics such as righteousness, holiness, and endurance depend upon the degree to which we have faith and character. Thus, you could say that Faith and Character are the common denominators (remember your fractions!) for most other biblical principles. It is often the case that no matter what topic you discuss, it won't be long before faith and/or character will be brought up. For this reason, I have chosen to focus on these two topics as representative of what God is attempting to do *IN US.*

FAITH

What is Faith?

Hebrews 11:1 defines faith and Hebrews 11:6 let's us know the importance of having faith toward God.

> *"Now faith is the <u>assurance</u> of things hoped for, the <u>conviction</u> of things not seen."* (Heb. 11:1, NASB)

"And without faith it is impossible to please Him, for he who comes to God <u>must believe that He is</u> and that <u>He is a rewarder</u> of those who seek Him." (Heb. 11:6, NASB)

From Hebrews 11:1 we see that faith involves *assurance* and *conviction*. Depending upon the translation, other terms may be used as substitutes for assurance and conviction such as *substance* and *evidence*. No matter what the term, the idea here is that faith is a type of **trust** and **reliance**. Trust in what? Reliance upon what? The answer to these questions is provided in Hebrews 11:6.

In Hebrews 11:6, we must trust in and rely upon two fundamental beliefs: 1) that God exists and 2) that He is a rewarder of those who seek Him. In a sense, the matching of vs. 1 and vs. 6 is reversed in order: the "assurance of things hoped for..." refers primarily to the fact that God is a "rewarder" and the "conviction of things not seen..." refers primarily to the notion that "He is." If we correctly match these verses, it should read something like: *We must have the conviction that although He is not seen, God is present. Furthermore, we should have the assurance that He will reward us with the things that we hope for* (Note: we must be careful to balance this last part with other scriptures in the Bible. In short, our assurance can only be firm when this hope is anchored in the will of God rather than our selfish motives of the flesh).

It is important to note that every challenge that we face in life is essentially an assault on the two fundamental beliefs listed above. When times are rough, our belief in the presence (i.e., 'existence') and favor (i.e., His propensity to reward) of God is threatened. Think about it! For this reason, every challenge we face is also an opportunity to strengthen our faith by strengthening these two beliefs. When God ultimately delivers us in our time of trouble, it reinforces and confirms the reality of both His presence and favor in our lives.

Building Faith

One of the most important things that God is currently attempting to do *IN US* is build our faith. While the Bible says that God has given each "a measure of faith" (Rom 12:3), faith is like a muscle that must be strengthened. We are all born with muscles. Some people are born naturally physiologically gifted with lean, strong muscles. However, most people have to exercise to get these physiques and muscles. The Bible speaks of people who have been given the "gift of faith" (1 Cor. 12:9). These are like those people who are naturally gifted physiologically; except they are *SUPERnaturally* gifted *SPIRITually* in the area of faith. While some of us might have the gift of faith as one of the giftings of the Holy Spirit, most of us have to build our faith through 'exercise.' Actually, even those with the gifting have to exercise their faith or that gifting will just be undeveloped and untapped potential.

In reality muscles are typically composed of muscle groups. That is, a group of smaller muscles form together to make up a bigger muscle. Faith is really a muscle group composed of at least three smaller muscles that must be developed in order to develop the overall muscle group of *Faith*. The first smaller muscle is the *belief that He is and that He is a rewarder*, as already discussed. However, this must produce the second part, which is *the ability to trust and rely upon Him*. Finally, when we can trust and rely upon Him this must produce the third part, which is *a firm obedience to His commands*. Bishop Raphael Green of Metro Christian Worship Center in St. Louis, MO. often refers to these three components of faith as *Insight, Agreement*, and *Obedience*: insight concerning the presence of God and His rewarding nature, agreement reflecting a decision to totally rely upon the insight that you received, and obedience to the commands and promptings of God.

As illustrated in the Figure 3.1 below, these smaller muscles are sequential in the order in which they are developed, meaning that each muscle is somewhat dependent upon the development of the muscle that precedes it. However, the Bible says that faith comes by hearing the word of God. So, now we are able to understand the crucial role that studying the Bible plays. In order to even begin to build the first muscle of our faith, we have to be exposed to and understand the word of God (i.e., the Bible).

Since reading the Bible is so crucial to developing our faith, I want to elaborate a little more on how the Bible builds faith. The more we are exposed to the word of God, the more we are exposed to ideas and thoughts that ***assume*** God's presence. This is in contrast to the overwhelming exposure that we have to secular ideas and experiences, which by the very definition of *Secularism* do not assume God's presence. Hence, reading the Bible reinforces a sense of God's presence, what I like to refer to as a "God Consciousness." This God Consciousness helps to establish His presence IN US.

Reading the Bible also reinforces our faith in the fact that He will reward us if we seek Him. We must understand that you can only have faith in something that has first been proven to be *faithful*. To be 'faithful' means to be reliable and dependable. Thus, only after something has been proven to be reliable and dependable, can we have faith in it. Well, in addition to reinforcing the presence of God or our God consciousness, the Bible reinforces the idea that "God is faithful" repeatedly. You can think of the 66 books of the Bible as 66 infomercials in which the faithfulness of God is being illustrated repeatedly. And like infomercials, the books of the Bible were designed not for just entertainment but rather to make you "want that" kind of relationship with God. So, when we read the Bible, we are in fact providing ourselves with the evidence and assurance of not only God's presence but also His faithfulness.

In sum, reading the Bible is the catalyst for developing our faith muscles. It reinforces our insight into the presence and faithfulness of the favor of God. To make our faith complete, we must come into agreement with this insight and be obedient to the principles and commands contained in it.

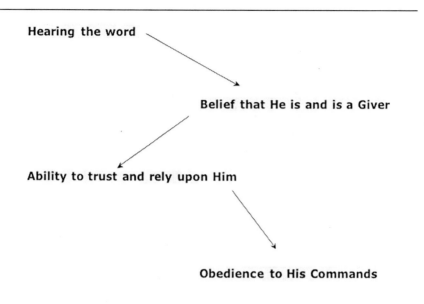

Figure 3.1 *Building muscles of Faith*

Finally, the development of Faith IN US is extremely important because 1) it is impossible to please God without Faith, and 2) everything else in our Christian walk depends upon our faith.

CHARACTER

What is character?

Character is the set of characteristics or virtues that could be used to describe the way we tend to deal with other people. These virtues represent a readiness to think or act in a certain way. Character drives both our initiation of actions (i.e., conversation or behavior) and the way that we respond to situations (e.g., emergencies, etc.).

Character has two important dimensions: Salience and Consistency. Something is only a part of our character (i.e., characteristic) if it is highly salient and highly consistent for us. *Salience* refers to the degree to which a particular virtue will be automatically used in a given situation. People differ in the salience of certain responses. For example, consider how you would respond immediately after an accident. Two responses are typical; both ironically involve invoking the name of God. Do you say "oh my God" or the other one (and you know the one!). Whichever response comes first can be said to be the most salient response. *Consistency* reflects the degree to which our response is the same across time and situations. Do you respond one way in one circumstance and another way under a different circumstance? So people can be distinguished in their characters by the degree to which God-like responses are automatic and consistent across situations and circumstances.

Why is character important?

It would take several books to fully discuss why character is so important for a Christian. So, let me provide a simple but important answer to the question of why character is important. Quite frankly, our character is the entity by which we do or do not reflect Jesus. It is important that we accurately represent Jesus to this world because the real key to evangelism is contained in Jesus' own words *"If I be lifted up, I'll draw all men unto me."* Thus, our job is to lift Him up by accurately reflecting His character to this world. This will be discussed at greater length in the next chapter. However, I want to say that we must reflect Jesus not just to be a witness to others but so that we can be a witness to ourselves as well. When we incorporate the attributes of God into ourselves we are, in fact, incorporating the ingredients that we need to live lives of inner peace, joy and righteousness. Thus, character is important because by reflecting Jesus we actually partake in His divine life and 'lift Him up' accurately before the world.

Building Character

To understand the character building process, we must first understand the concept of **salvation** better. Salvation is both instant and a process. That is, we are born again and are guaranteed access to Heaven immediately upon our sincere acceptance and confession of Jesus as Lord (i.e., ruler of our lives). This is the gift of Salvation that we cannot earn through works of our own. Furthermore, we receive our giftings of the Spirit also instantly. Although it needs to be cultivated, our calling to be prophets, teachers, etc. is already in us at our new birth into Christ. In addition to our calling, the various gifts used in that calling (e.g., words of knowledge, healing, faith, etc.) are also made available to us at our new birth.

The Bible also teaches that there is a process dimension to our salvation (see 1 Cor. 1:18; Phil. 2:12, 13, 1 Pet. 1:9, 2:2). For example, Paul exhorts the church in Philippi to *"...continue to work out your salvation with fear and trembling..."* Peter exhorts the church to crave spiritual milk so that you *"may grow up in your salvation."* This process dimension of salvation has often been confused with meaning that we have to somehow work for the gift and giftings of salvation discussed above. A more careful study of the scriptures makes it clear that the *process of salvation* refers not to our spiritual condition or status with God, but rather to our character.

You may have noticed that you did not necessarily immediately stop having bad thoughts, desiring bad things, or even having bad feelings on the day/night you got saved. God does want your thoughts, desires, and feelings to ultimately conform to His standards. But, this is a process. It takes time. This process is the greatest miracle that you will ever witness. The transformation of your character from a selfish/self-centered one to a God-centered one defies psychological explanations. So what God has done FOR US is not merely a matter of getting into heaven, but paving the way for you to develop the character that leads to a better *quality* of life. As you will see, developing character is the primary objective of what God is doing IN US.

While I will deal with the subject of THROUGH US in the next chapter, I must note that it is our character that makes us distinctive as Christians and not our prosperity, as some seem to be suggesting in the body of Christ today. Please consider that if Bill Gates, Warren Buffet, or Donald Trump woke up tomorrow morning with all the money combined of all the preachers who boast about their prosperity, they would probably jump out of a window! Quite frankly, the prosperity of the church does not impress the world. If anything, it has made the world more suspicious of the church. Please don't get me wrong, I do believe that God desires to prosper and *does prosper* His church. God may even ultimately utilize things such as our prosperity to get the world's attention, but the real key to our witness is *the degree to which our character reflects the nature of Jesus.* I believe that's why the Apostle John wished that all other forms of our prosperity be in proximity to the prosperity of our souls (3 John 1:2).

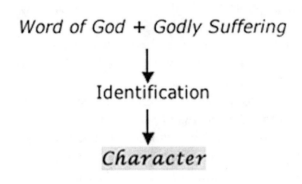

Figure 3.2 *Developing Godly Character*

Identification with Jesus: the key to building character

Character is developed primarily through our identification with Jesus. As the formula presented in Figure 3.2 suggests, the intersection of the word of God and suffering will produce identification with the character of Jesus. By *intersection* here, I am referring to the idea that suffering be viewed through the lens of the word of God. Suffering can be viewed either from a worldly perspective or a Godly perspective. When suffering is viewed from a worldly perspective, it often leads to hopelessness and despair. However, when suffering is viewed from a Godly perspective, it leads to identification with Jesus. In this sense, identification plays the role of a mediator between this intersection (i.e., Word-Suffering) and character.

To identify with something or someone is to "take on" the same characteristics as the entity that you are identifying with. In other words, your self-concept is transformed such that it conforms to whatever you are identifying with. You eventually start to describe yourself using the same adjectives and characteristics that you would use to describe that entity: *Person X is kind, nice, and friendly and so am I.*

Likewise, identification with Jesus means that our self-concept becomes conformed to His image. We lose distinctions between His ways and our own. Who He is, is who we are (or at least, who we want to be!). This is really what the word *"Christian"* is supposed to stand for. The early church was given this label by outsiders because they *were identified with* (i.e., acted and talked like) Jesus Christ!

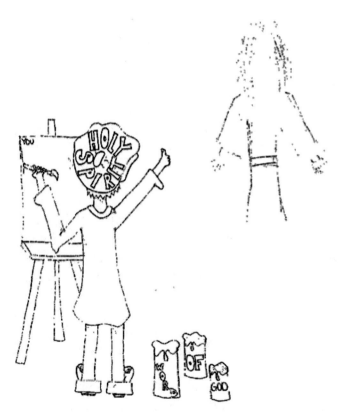

Figure 3.3 The Holy Spirit, the Word of God, and You

Understanding *how* the word of God and godly suffering establishes identification with Him is the key to building character. So, we will review each of the these concepts in turn:

Word of God. The importance of the word of God in helping to establish our character is illustrated in figure 3.3. In this figure we see a painter beginning to paint a model on a piece of canvas. The painting process depicted here is analogous to the process of how the word of God is used to establish character. Note that the objects in this picture are labeled such that the canvas represents us (i.e., our souls), the painter is the Holy Spirit, the model is Jesus, and the paint is the Word of God. So we can interpret this picture to reflect the actions of the Holy Spirit attempting to reproduce the image of Jesus IN US. But, what is absolutely essential to the whole process is paint (i.e., the word of God). Without paint, the painter is only stroking the canvas with a dry brush. This is ironically descriptive of where a lot of people are in their spiritual development. They are getting pleasant and ticklish "strokes" on Sundays, but no real transference and transformation are occurring. Only when the word of God (i.e., the paint) is present, can the Holy Spirit reproduce the image and character of Christ IN US. So, whenever we study the word of God, we basically give the Holy Spirit the paint that He needs to impart the character of Christ on the canvass of our souls.

Suffering. In addition to the word of God, suffering is also crucial to our character. Some teach that suffering is correlated with a lack or absence of faith. However, the Bible says that all who live godly will suffer (2 Tim. 3:12). So far from being something that we can avoid totally, the Bible invites us to partake in the fellowship of Jesus' suffering.

The character development that the word of God initiates IN US is then tested and refined by suffering. Romans 5:3,4 makes it clear that our patient endurance of suffering will produce character. Why? Because varying our life from good times to bad times is a way of testing the consistency or steadfastness of the virtues or ingredients of character in our life. Is *love, gentleness, goodness*, and *meekness* displayed just as much in the bad times in our life as in the good times? This is a way of testing the salience and consistency that Christ's character has been able to take in us.

The role of suffering in the assessment and development of character is also analogous to weight training. Weight training involves both assessment and development. If a person were to attempt to lift 150 pounds as many times as he or she could, two things would be happening. For one, they would be learning some important information about how much weight they could lift and how many times they could lift it (assessment). Secondly, that person would be actually developing their muscles and increasing their ability to lift weights in the future (development). Suffering has a similar function. People get an assessment of their "spiritual growth" by learning how much they can bear, while at the same time actually developing the ability to bear more with each trial and tribulation.

There are two kinds of suffering: *Disciplined suffering* and *Crisis Suffering*. Disciplined suffering is proactive or voluntary in nature. In other words, it is intentional on the part of the person. People voluntarily submit themselves to a process that is going to make them suffer. Sound strange? Not really! That's what physical exercise is. Working out doesn't feel good while you are doing it. Your muscles are being stretched, ripped, and even drained. Your body is suffering. Yet, we voluntarily do it. Why? We do it because of the benefits it has for developing and shaping our bodies, which may take a while to materialize.

There are also some voluntary spiritual exercises that we do to develop our character. Studying the word of God, prayer, fellowship, and fasting are a few examples. Fasting is actually a very good example of a disciplined suffering exercise. When you fast, you voluntarily exercise the pre-eminence of God above and beyond your own desires. It is mostly mental because, unlike starving, you actually have food available that you could eat, but choose not to. Fasting and dieting are not the same thing either because, unlike dieting, fasting is not just the act of resisting food. It is really about focusing on and discerning the will of God. Fasting is a powerful spiritual exercise because it actually combines both elements of character development: the word of God and suffering. So, fasting can be considered a form of disciplined suffering.

In contrast to disciplined suffering, crisis suffering is *reactive* in nature. It is unintentional and usually unexpected or accidental.

Financial lack, weather disasters, car accidents, physical ailments, and even death are all examples of crisis suffering. Crisis suffering comes from the emergencies in our lives. Our character is also tested and developed during these times as well. However, the ideal situation is that we are better prepared for such emergencies by having engaged in disciplined suffering ahead of time. Nowadays the primary purpose for building muscle is just to look good, but before we had the technology we have now, the purpose was to be ready for an emergency in which you might have to lift or move some heavy weight. Nevertheless, crisis suffering establishes the faithfulness of God in us as discussed above and so helps us to identify with His Character. So, James was not exactly crazy when he exhorted us to "consider it all joy" when we face crises, because as he also mentions, such testing will eventually produce a maturity and completeness of character IN US (James 1:2-4).

Returning to the model presented in figure 3.2, perhaps now we can see how suffering, the word of God, and identification all combine to produce character. We must understand that it is really our ability to *see Him for who He is and what He does* (i.e., identification) that is the key to making sure that our times of suffering produce real character. It is possible to suffer for nothing.

We can go through times of suffering and yet never seek after and see God.

This is suffering for nothing because we miss the opportunity for character development that comes from seeking and identifying with God. In case you missed it, this was really Job's epiphany (great revelation!) at the end of his time of suffering. In Job 42:5, Job says *"I have <u>heard</u> of you by the hearing of the ear; But now my eye <u>sees</u> You"* (NASB). God didn't allow the devil to destroy all the stuff that Job owned just so He could prove a point to the devil only; nor was the story just about prospering Job with more stuff. There was a benefit in this story for Job! God seized an opportunity to develop Job's character by allowing Job to graduate to a level above merely just hearing about God to actually "seeing" and hence, identifying with God.

Why do we need to know this and what do we do with this info?

Both *faith* and *character* are in essence our soul muscles. Notice I didn't say "spiritual" muscles. It was intentional. The Bible teaches that our spirits are born-again 'perfect' (Hebrews 10:14; 12:23). And because YOU are a spirit, YOU are perfect. However, you possess a soul and live in a body. They are not immediately made perfect, but must be developed *through* the salvation that comes immediately to our spirits. Likewise, Faith and Character are not perfected in the born again believer. Being a part of the soul, they must be developed. The strength of our faith and character depends upon our *will-ingness* to invest in the development of our *thoughts* and *feelings.* Notice that the will, thoughts, and feelings are *mental* processes, not spiritual. Nevertheless, their development will depend heavily upon the degree to which we put them under the control of our spirit.

One of the most misunderstood concepts in Christianity is the notion of "spiritual growth." The term itself does not actually appear anywhere in the Bible, but is consistently implied, especially in passages like 1 Corinthians 3:2 and 1 Peter 2:2. Spiritual growth is not the growth of the "spirit" per se, but rather growth in the degree to which the spirit rules the soul and the body. So, given that we have been talking about Faith and Character in this chapter, we could say that spiritual growth actually reflects both the degree to which our faith is in the presence and favor of God and the degree to which our character is saturated with the fruits of the spirit. Therefore, you should make up your mind right now to submit both your physical body and your mental processes (i.e., will, thoughts, feelings) to the rule of your spirit (which is under the rule of the Holy Spirit).

It is clear that both Faith and Character are developed through exercise, more specifically, 'resistance' training. Studying and meditating on the word of God, praying, and attending church are all forms of spiritual resistance training. As discussed earlier, fasting is a particularly good technique inasmuch as we allow our obedience to God to overcome the resistance posed by our hunger. Furthermore, learning to embrace times of suffering is also a form of resistance training. There is no natural instinct to embrace suffering, but yet, we learn to endure it for the moment. This is why James 1:2 told us to "count it all joy" when we face trials. We don't count it joy because of the suffering per se, but rather because of what our endurance of the suffering will ultimately produce: faith and character.

Like muscles, faith is developed by being used (i.e., the operation of faith). As discussed earlier, Bishop Raphael Green suggests that the operation of faith involves three essential components: Insight, Agreement, and Obedience. First, we must receive insight from the word of God. Insight about what God has done for us (...His faithfulness), what God is presently doing in us, what God wants to do through us, and then ultimately what God plans to do to us (our ultimate hope). So in a sense, the very reading of this book is building the first ingredient of faith (insight!). This is why the Bible says that faith comes by hearing (and hearing and hearing....). Second, we must accept or come into agreement with the insight of the Bible. To come into agreement with the Bible is to 1) recognize its value and relevance, and 2) to embrace its rules and principles as your own. This can be tough! It often calls for the abandonment of ideas that we have developed from our own experience, education, and authorities that are in contradiction to God's word. The final step in the operation of faith is to be obedient to the insight that you have agreed with. The Apostle James wrote that faith without works was dead (James 2:26). Thus, the faith process isn't usually complete until it results in some form of action or at least decision.

The key word for how you should respond to what God is trying to do IN YOU is <u>submission</u>. You must submit to His divine work in your life. It is designed to develop and cultivate both your faith and character. So make a mental decision right now to seize and embrace opportunities, whether voluntarily (e.g., fasting) or non-voluntarily (e.g., trials), for building your faith and character. Also, practice the three steps to walking in faith on a daily basis, especially during your faith and character building opportunities: 1) receive *Insight* through a careful and consistent study time in God's word, 2) *Agree* with God's word by meditating on it and incorporating it into your value system, and 3) *Obey* God's word by using it as your guide for taking action and criteria for making decisions!

Chapter 4

Through Us

All this is from God, who reconciled us to himself through Christ and gave us the <u>ministry of reconciliation</u>: that God was reconciling the world to himself in Christ, not counting men's sins against them. And He has committed to us the message of reconciliation. We are therefore Christ's <u>ambassadors</u>, as though God were making His appeal **through us**. *We implore you on Christ's behalf: Be reconciled to God.* (2 Corinthians 5:18-20)

But thanks be to God, who always leads us in triumphal procession in Christ and **through us** *spreads everywhere the fragrance of the <u>knowledge of him.</u>* (2 Corinthians 2:14; NIV)

The Bible analogizes the church in many ways...the Branches (Jn. 15:5), the Bride (Rev. 21:2, 9), Children (Rom. 8:16), the Body of Christ (Eph. 4:12), Salt (Matt: 5:13), Light (Matt. 5:14), etc. For the most part, these analogies refer either to our relationship to Christ or our relationship to the world. For example, branches, bride, and body all refer to our relationship to Christ, whereas, salt and light refer to our relationship to the world. This chapter focuses on the latter. Of course, our relationship to the world is only appropriately balanced when our relationship to Christ is primary and in tact.

All of the analogies for the church's relationship to the world can be summed up in one: <u>Ambassadorship</u>. As the passage listed above makes it clear, the church has been called to ambassadorship. We are most familiar with the natural usage of this term rather than its biblical usage. However, there are many aspects of the natural usage that nicely illustrate many of the spiritual realities of the church's ambassadorship in the world. So let's first consider some natural definitions of an ambassador:

- "A diplomatic official of the highest rank sent by one country as its long-term representative to another." (Encarta® World English Dictionary © 1999 Microsoft Corporation)
- "An ambassador... is a diplomatic official accredited to a foreign sovereign or government, or to an international organization, to serve as the official representative of his or her own country. In everyday usage it applies to the ranking plenipotentiary minister stationed in a foreign capital. The host country typically allows the ambassador control of a specific territory called an embassy, whose territory, staff, and even vehicles are generally afforded diplomatic immunity from most laws of the host country." (Wikipedia online encyclopedia)

The idea of ambassadorship provides the umbrella for a number of principles that speak to our role and conduct in the world until Jesus comes:

<u>Exiles in a foreign land</u>. It is important to every Christian to remember that this world is not our home. The Bible regards us as strangers (i.e., a peculiar people). However, it is important to recognize that our call is not to become "separatists" in the natural sense. God wants us in and among the world. During their Babylonian captivity, God instructed the Jews to become integrated and involved in Babylon and even pray for that city. I believe God has instructed Christians to do likewise: become involved and integrated into our cities, states, and nations. More importantly, He wants us to pray

for all three as well. So, God does not want us to be separatists in the physical, but He does want us to be separatists spiritually and mentally (Note: this is what it means to be 'holy,' or 'set apart'). So, God wants us to be separatists in our outlook and values. He does not want us to look upon this world as our 'home.'

Diplomatic immunity. One of the most interesting and some-times controversial issues around ambassadors is that they have what is called *diplomatic immunity*. Diplomatic immunity means that ambassadors are not subject to the legal systems of the host country. Historically, some ambassadors have used this to literally get away with murder. They don't even have to pay taxes to the host country. To the Christian, the Bible says that although we do live in the world, we are not *of* this world (John 15:19; 17:14-16). Moreover, it says that we are not to be subject to the principles of this world (Col. 2:8, 20). Now, that doesn't mean that we should stop paying our taxes and ignore the speed limit. They will take our stuff away and put us in jail! It means that we are not to be subject to the world's outlook and philosophy about life, which is generally one that does not acknowledge and submit to God. It can have physical implications as well. Even when this world (i.e., host nation) might be experiencing physical calamities and economic downturns, God may still protect and prosper us, His nation.

Sovereign property. Related somewhat to diplomatic immunity is the fact that any and all properties belonging to the ambassador are considered sovereign property. Ambassadors live in what are called *embassies*. Although these embassies might physically sit in the host nation, the host nation cannot trespass onto the grounds of these embassies without a declaration of war. The possessions that Christ has given to us to do His bidding belong to Him regardless of the fact that they reside on this planet. Personally, I consider my home, car, everything I own, and even myself to be the sovereign and exclusive property of the Kingdom of God. When demonic forces stir up trouble, it is my job to inform them that they are trespassing on sovereign territory and must leave.

Mediators. Ambassadors are mediators between both the nation that they are representing and the host nation. As a mediator, their job is to basically represent and relay messages back and forth between the two nations. As Christians, we have this same function. We must relay messages back and forth between God and the world. We do this by evangelism and intercession. As discussed below, evangelism is basically the process by which we relay *the* message from God to the world, while intercession is the process by which we relay messages from the world to God.

Ministry of Reconciliation: Evangelism and Intercession

The lead verse in this chapter (2 Corinthians 5:18-20) pointed out the fact that as ambassadors we have been handed the *ministry of reconciliation*. As mediators, our primary business in the host nation (i.e., the world) concerns Jesus' desire to have the host nation restored to relationship and fellowship with Him. As briefly mentioned above, the two tools that we have to carryout this ministry are *evangelism* and *intercession*.

Figure 4.1 *Relationship of Ambassador to the Origin and Host Nations.*

Evangelism. From the ambassador's perspective, evangelism is the act of establishing relations between the host nation and the nation of origin. As the verse listed above from 2 Corinthians 5:18-20 notes, our message from the Kingdom of God to the world is the message of reconciliation. Through us, God wants the world to know that He wants a covenantal relationship (or what in ambassador talk is called "diplomatic relations") with them. We not only express His desire but also His strategy for bringing this covenantal relationship about: Jesus. Like John said, we *"...testify that the Father has sent the Son to be the Savior of the world"* (1 John 4:14). So, evangelism is how we communicate God's plan for reconciliation.

Intercession. From the ambassador's perspective, intercession is the act of relaying the needs and concerns of the host country back to the ruler of the nation of origin. For example, ambassadors play key roles in getting US aid and assistance for the host countries that they are in. Spiritually speaking, intercession is prayer made on behalf of other people. The Bible says that we ought to intercede for the rulers of this world (see 1 Timothy 2:1,2). When we intercede, we present the needs of the world to God. Of course, the greatest need of people in this world happens to be exactly what the message of reconciliation is all about: the need for relationship and fellowship with Jesus Christ.

In summary, as mediators and ambassadors of *goodwill* (i.e., because it is HIS will), we utilize the strategy of evangelism to put forth the message of reconciliation. This message is the tool that Jesus uses to make His appeal *through us* to the world to come back to a loving and devoted relationship with Him. Also, we utilize the strategy of intercession to call for divine intervention and aid from God on behalf of this world.

Why do we need to know this and what do we do with this info?

The message of reconciliation is not merely a verbal presentation, but also one of conduct. Phil. 2:15 says *"...prove yourselves to be blameless and innocent, children of God above reproach in the midst of a crooked and perverse generation, among whom you appear as lights in the world."* Furthermore 2 Cor. 9:13 says that *"...they will glorify God for your obedience to your confession of the gospel of Christ and for the liberality of your contribution to them and to all."* Thus, it is clear that the message that God wants to deliver through us is just as much in our conduct as it is in our lips. So, an accurate representation of Jesus' character (as discussed in the last chapter) is crucial to our ability to serve as ambassadors and deliver the message of reconciliation with Christ.

The key word for how you need to respond to what God is trying to do THROUGH you is cooperation. That is, you must attempt to cooperate with the flow of the Holy Spirit as an ambassador of

Christ. A few steps that you ought to follow to cooperate with the spirit of God are presented below.

The first thing that you need to do is construct an image of yourself as an "*ambassador for the Kingdom of God.*" This should change not only the way that you see yourself, but also the way that you see your *purpose* and *role* in the earth. No matter what your individual calling or gifting is it flows out of your primary calling as an *ambassador for Christ*. Even if you don't know what your specific calling is yet, start there: you are an ambassador of the Kingdom of God!

Secondly, meditate on each of the principles associated with being an ambassador discussed above: exiles, mediators, immunity, and sovereign property. Such meditation will change the way that you see the things around you. For example, your house is not just a house; it is an embassy of the kingdom of God. So, stop allowing the devil to trespass on what is supposed to be "sovereign property" of the Kingdom of God.

Thirdly, to be a good ambassador, you obviously have to be familiar with the principles of the nation that you are representing. Spiritually speaking, you have to be familiar with the principles of the Kingdom of God. Since, those principles are presented in the Bible, you have to diligently study it so that you may be thoroughly equipped (2 Tim. 3:16) as you attempt to accurately handle the word of truth (2 Tim. 2:15) in presenting the principles of the Kingdom of God to the world. So, make up your mind that you are going to study the word of God, not only because of what God is doing IN you (i.e., last chapter), but also because of what He wants to do THROUGH you!

Finally, remember that your primary tools as an ambassador for bringing about the ministry of reconciliation is *evangelism* and *intercession*. So, commit yourself to the practices of evangelism and intercession. In other words share the gospel and pray for people. As an evangelist and an intercessor you serve as a mediator between God and the world, and ultimately bear some level of responsibility for establishing relations between the two.

Chapter 5

To Us

Then I saw a new heaven and a new earth, for the first heaven and the first earth had passed away, and there was no longer any sea. I saw the Holy City, the New Jerusalem coming down out of heaven from God, prepared as a bride beautifully dressed for her husband. And I heard a loud voice from the throne saying, "Now the dwelling of God is with men, and He will live with them. They will be His people, and God himself will be with them and be their God. He will wipe every tear from their eyes. There will be no more death or mourning or crying or pain, for the old order of things has passed away...I am making everything new... It is done. I am the Alpha and the Omega the Beginning and the End. To him who is thirsty I will give to drink without cost from the spring of the water of life. He who overcomes will inherit all this, and I will be His God and He will be my son."
(Rev. 21: 1-7)

This passage reflects the ultimate destiny of the person who puts Jesus in control of their life. There are a variety of eschatological (i.e., end of times) views and interpretations. For the most part, theologians tend to agree more on *WHAT* events will occur than *WHEN*, or the sequence, in which these events will occur. For this reason, there are as many perspectives on the end-times as there are theologians studying them. However, all truly born again scholars agree that we all end up where the passage above (Rev. 21: 1-7) describes. So differences in eschatology are really differences in how people see us getting to this point, but we all agree that we GET to this point.

There is a lot of information in the Bible about the end-times. In the Old Testament, several books (Daniel and Ezekiel in particular) make prophetic utterances about the end times. In the New Testament, the gospel books (i.e., Mathew, Mark, Luke, John) record several of Jesus' utterances about the end times. Also 1st Corinthians chapter 15, and 1st and 2nd Thessalonians all record what God revealed to and through the Apostle Paul concerning the end times. Finally, most readers are aware of the heavy concentration of end-time topics revealed to the Apostle John in the book of Revelation. So the *end-times* are persistent and important topics in the word of God.

Frankly, people normally begin to break out in uncontrolled yawning whenever end-times are talked about. For this reason, it is probably the least preached and taught topic in the church today. Some Christians even avoid the topic out of fear (i.e., fear of the unknown). However, there is no reason to fear the end-times.

Despite the lack of overall clarity, the main point of end-times teaching is very clear and agreed upon: **JESUS WINS, and SO DO WE**! It's all the other details about *how*, *where*, and *when* that we're not sure about and therefore tend to differ in opinion. But the *what* (i.e., He wins-We win) and *why* (i.e., because God planned it that way before the foundation of the earth) are clear! Thus, if we get these two points, we are getting the essence of it all. Furthermore, if we will truly embrace the **what** and the **why**, we will be prepared to participate in the **how**, and be **where** we need to be **when** the time comes. So there's no need to fear the end times. In fact, the Apostle Peter says that we ought to *"...look forward to the day of God and speed its coming"* (2 Pet. 3:12).

This chapter is about the end times, but more about the *what* and *why* than the *how, where*, and *when*. The *what* and *why* really speak about our ultimate destiny of what God aims to do TO US, and that is to *Glorify* us and bring us into *His Rest*.

GLORY AND GLORIFICATION

The term "glory" typically refers to the brightness, radiance or fame of something. To glorify something typically means to attribute honor or fame to it. Ironically, glorification can have two separate meanings when applied to man versus God. To glorify *man* can often represent the giving of exaggerated or undue honor or fame. Thus, man's glory is often vain and fake. However, with God, glory does not represent an undue radiance or fame, but His essential character. Thus, to glorify God means to reveal God for who He really is. Nineteenth century evangelist Charles Finney said that God's glory is "...*the showing forth, the revealing, the manifesting the glory of His character—his essential glory—to His creatures: the laying open His glory to the apprehension of intelligences.*"

God's glory is the awesomeness and excellence of His multiple perfect manifestations. It is an attempt to put into words what God is like. And yet, no one set of words can comprehensively describe the totality of His magnificence and holiness. God's glory might be described by referring to His deeds of power, mercy, grace, justice and love. But the truth is that His deeds are only reflections of who He is. Pastor John Piper of Bethlehem Baptist Church put it this way: "God's glory is the perfect harmony of all His attributes into one infinitely beautiful and personal being."

The great thing about studying God's glory is that you actually get back to God's main objective. If you have ever wondered "what is it all about?" then you should seek to understand what God wants to do TO US and, more specifically, you should seek to understand His glory. God's plan, which originated before the foundation of the earth and the creation of humankind, is based upon His glory.

We were created to live our lives such that they would reflect God's glory. Said another way, we were created from the beginning in God's image so that we might *image forth God's glory* (Ephesians 2:7-10). Furthermore, humankind was commanded to multiply and fill the earth so that the knowledge of the glory of God would cover the sea: *For the earth will be filled with the knowledge of the glory of the LORD, as the waters cover the sea* (Habakkuk 2:14). Thus, we are challenged by Paul to "Whether you eat or drink or whatever you do, do all *to the glory of God*" (1 Cor. 10:31). Jesus himself said "Let your light so shine among men that they may see your good deeds and *give glory to your Father* in heaven" (Mt. 5:16). So, you see, it is all about His glory! Humankind was created for God's glory, Jesus came to be the physical manifestation of God's glory (Heb. 1:3), and the church is commanded to do all that we do for God's glory.

The most notable leaders in the Bible are arguably Moses, David, and Paul. And one attribute that they all held in common was a desire to see the glory of God. Moses' prayer to see the glory of God is recorded in Ex. 33: 12-23. David's desire to dwell in the manifested glory of God is recorded in Ps 27:4. Finally, Paul's petition to know Him in the glory of His power and suffering is listed in Phil 3:10. These mature men of God realized somewhere in their walk with God that to personally experience the manifested presence of God is the ultimate experience a person could have.

Our ultimate destiny is to have the presence of God fully revealed to us. Second Thessalonians 1:10 speaks about the second coming of Christ as that "…day He comes to be *glorified* in His holy people and to be marveled at among all those who have believed." Please note that this is not just a mere manifestation of God in our presence, but also a complete manifestation of God in our very beings (i.e., In Us). Hence, we will be glorified with Him (Rom. 8:17) in the sense that we will be completely transformed to reflect His nature (i.e., His glory) in our thoughts, speech, actions, and appearance. Thus, when the Bible talks about the transformation of our mortal physical bodies to immortal spiritual bodies, it is signaling our ultimate glorification.

Romans 8:30 suggests that our glorification is the final stage of the process that began with our *predestination* (see Figure 5.1). Whereas our predestination, calling, and justification are now past tense concepts, as we discovered in the chapter on FOR US, our glorification is currently a process. That is, we are currently being transformed to reflect His image or presence from glory to glory (2 Cor. 3:17-18). However, one day, God will complete this process and we will be totally transformed and merged into His glory. On that day, the whole world will understand what Paul wrote in Rom.

11:36 (NIV): "For from Him and through Him and to Him are all things. To Him be the glory forever! Amen."

Predestined → **Called** → **Justified** → **Glorified**

Figure 5.1 *Stages of Glorification*

REST

¹Therefore, since the promise of entering His rest still stands, let us be careful that none of you be found to have fallen short of it.³ ...Now we who have believed enter that rest... ⁹There remains, then, a Sabbath-rest for the people of God; ¹⁰for anyone who enters God's rest also rests from His own work, just as God did from his. ¹¹Let us, therefore, make every effort to enter that rest, so that no one will fall by following their example of disobedience. (Hebrews 4:1, 3, 9-11)

Like the concept of glorification, the idea of a Sabbath-rest is also a process that has an ultimate conclusion when Jesus returns. When we accepted Jesus as the ruler of our lives, we then rested from the labor of attempting to earn salvation on our own. Nevertheless, we are still in the process of walking in righteousness (i.e., both IN US and THROUGH US). Thus, we have both entered God's rest and are still awaiting His ultimate rest (this principle is often called "dynamic tension" in theological circles). God's ultimate rest will be when we no longer even have to struggle to live righteously; instead it will become natural to us because of our transformed nature.

Hopefully, you can now see the connection between our glorification and entering into the ultimate rest in God. When our time is up, we will be merged into God's glory such that our mortal souls and bodies will be transformed. Then, living godly will no longer be a struggle because we will be completely delivered from the demonic and fleshly temptations that pull us away from righteousness.

Glory and Rest go hand-in-hand as the ultimate destiny and goal of what God will do TO US as believers. An early indicator of this was God's answer to Moses' request that God reveal His ways to him. God's response is recorded in Exodus 33:14 "And He said, 'my presence shall go with you, and I will give you rest.'" Herein we see God promising Moses both a revelation of His glory (i.e., His presence) and His rest.

Why do we need to know this and what do we do with this info?

The simple answer to why it is important to know what God will do TO US at the end of times is because 1) it let's us know the overall objective and 2) it provides us hope. As we ponder the future of what God will do TO US, we must fix our hope on our coming *Glorification* in Him. It is more than a "pie-in-the-sky" fantasy. It is a coming reality. Then we shall see Him as He is and our transformation will be made complete. This is really the main objective: that we would ultimately be conformed into His image and worship Him.

Hope is absolutely essential to our Christian walk. For one, faith is based upon it. Also, the absence of hope leads to despair, depression, and even suicide. Knowing that these ragged bodies that we have and this dysfunctional world that we live in is not all there is, is our primary motivation for continuing in this life. It is our buffer against the fear of death. You see, *death*, in ambassador lingo (last chapter), is merely returning to our home nation.

Because hope is so essential, the key word for how you should respond to what God has planned to do TO you is <u>expectation</u>. You should have an earnest expectation of His ultimate glorification and rest. Now, when you have an earnest expectation of something, you prepare for it. When you are expecting a baby, you don't wait for the baby to arrive before you put things in order. No, you typically have the baby shower and fix up the room *before* the baby arrives. Thus, your earnest expectation of what Christ will do TO US is indicated by the amount of effort that you put into preparing for it. Prepare for His ultimate glorification now by making your personal objective to live your life to manifest His glory everywhere you go, in everything you do! Also, prepare for His rest by working! Rest always feels better when it comes after a long hard time of labor, whereby you can sit back and look at what you have accomplished. Get busy! Look for opportunities to display God's glory, beginning in and through your local church.

Chapter 6

A CONCEPTUAL TOOL

As I stated in the preface, this book introduces the four dimensions of the ministry of Christ to ultimately encourage people to become better disciples of our Lord Jesus Christ. However, the four dimensions, because they serve as a conceptual tool (i.e., a way to categorize information), can also be used as an important Bible study tool.

As a Bible study tool, these four dimensions can be used as a context in which to understand individual passages and as a way to study particular topics. As a context, verses can be sorted into the four dimensions by considering whether the verse is 1) past tense about what's already been accomplished by the grace of God (FOR US), 2) present tense about how God is developing our faith and/or character traits (IN US), 3) present tense about how God wants to use us (THROUGH US), or 4) future tense about the conclusion of things (TO US). Each dimension provides a context by which passages in the Bible can be better understood.

Using the four dimensions to study a particular topic involves using them as a guide for finding information on a given topic. Many topics have verses in the Bible on them representing all four dimensions (see Table 6.1 below). Thus, we should learn to look for all four dimensions on a topic and not just focus on verses from just one dimension. Even when all four dimensions cannot be found explicitly in the text of the Bible, the wisdom of God can be used to speculate on what the other dimensions might be. Thus, the four dimensions can serve as a conceptual tool for understanding various topics in the Bible.

There are many debates that could be resolved if people understood how to use this conceptual tool in their study. Many debates tend to exaggerate the extremes of an issue and therefore, tend to represent "either/or" forms of thinking. However, because there are four dimensions to the ministry of Christ, the answers to many questions raised in these debates are not of the "either/or" variety but of the "both/and."

Allow me to illustrate what I mean by the "either/or" and "both/and" distinction by invoking a very classic story about some blind men and an elephant. Although this story appears to have originated in India, it has accrued several different versions to it. In most versions, a group of blind men touch an elephant to learn what it is like. Each one touches a different part such as the side, leg or the tusk. Each one touches a different part such as the side, leg or the tusk. When they compare notes on what they felt, they find that they are in complete disagreement about the nature of an elephant. The man who is feeling the trunk argues that an elephant is a long narrow thing. On the other hand, the man who is feeling the side says no, an elephant is a big and massive creature. Still the other men, who are feeling different parts of the elephant, each assert a different description.

This story has been used as a basis for the doctrines of pluralism and relativism to suggest that reality may be viewed differently depending upon one's perspective. I am not using it in this way because I don't believe that truth is pluralistic or relative. Our ability as mortal human beings to understand truth may be somewhat pluralistic or relative. But these conditions are neither impenetrable nor unavoidable. The universal and fixed truth of Jesus Christ can penetrate our fleshly and limited abilities. So, I do not believe in the pluralism or relativism of truth.

Table 6.1 **Key Biblical Scriptures in the Four Dimensions**

	FOR US	**IN US**	**THROUGH US**	**TO US**
Salvation	Acts 16:31 Rom 8:24 Eph. 2:5,8	1 Cor. 1:18 Phil 2:12 1 Pet. 1:9	Acts 13:47 1 Cor. 9:22 1 Cor. 10:33	Heb. 9:28 1 Peter 1:5 Rev. 12:10
Sanctified/ Holiness	Acts 20:32 1 Cor. 6:11 Heb. 10:10	Rom. 6: 19 2 Cor. 7:1 1 Thess 4:4	1 Cor. 7:14 1 Timothy 4:5 2 Pet. 3:11	1 Cor. 15:51 1 Thess. 3:13 1 Thess. 5:23
Justifica tion/Right- eousness	Rom. 5:9 Rom. 10:10 1 Cor. 6:11	Rom. 6:13 2 Tim. 2:22 1 John 3:10	2 Cor. 5:21 2 Cor. 6:7 2 Timothy 3:16	Galatians 5:5 2 Tim 4:8 2 Peter 3:13

I do, however, believe the story of the elephant and the blind men is analogous to the fact that many of the main doctrinal truths of the Bible are multi-dimensional. More specifically, these doctrinal truths tend to have the four dimensions discussed in this book. Thus, many biblical debates resemble the story of the blind men and the elephant. The reality is that they may all be touching on a different dimension of biblical truth and thus, the correct answer isn't neces- sarily that one is more correct than the other (i.e., either/or) but rather that both are correct (i.e., both/and).

Examples of what I am talking about are endless. Thus, there isn't enough space to discuss them all. So, allow me to tackle the one that I think is perhaps the most crucial debate of them all: *Salvation.* Salvation is the crux of Christianity. Without it, there's no reason for what we Christians are doing. There's no reason for me to write this book, or you, the reader, to be reading it. Therefore, we would have to conclude that settling the issue of salvation is of the utmost importance.

What does the Bible say about Salvation? Consider the diversity of these scriptures:

- For in this hope *we were saved...* (Romans 8:24)
- ...but to us who *are being saved* it is the power of God. (1 Cor. 1:18)
- ...that *you may bring salvation* to the ends of the earth. (Acts 13:47)
- ... until **the** *coming of the salvation* that is ready to be revealed in the last time. (1 Peter 1:5)

At first glance, each of these verses appears to be saying something quite different about the nature and status of salvation. It could get confusing. Are we saved already, being saved, or won't be saved until Jesus comes back? Any doctrine built around only one of these verses is likely to assert only one of the options that I just presented. However, in reality, there is no need for a choice. All of them are equally correct. Each of these verses reflects a different dimension of salvation (see Table 6.1): Romans 8:24 – FOR US; 1 Corinthians 1:18 – IN US; Acts 13:47 – THROUGH US; 1 Peter 1:5 TO US. Thus, any doctrine of salvation that is built around only one of these verses is incomplete.

The failure to understand and appreciate all four dimensions of what the Bible has to say about *Salvation* has led to some rather unbalanced perspectives on the status of our salvation. For example, those who just focus on those scriptures that address the FOR US dimension correctly acknowledge our status as righteous before God with guaranteed access into heaven. However, by ignoring the other dimensions of salvation, they fail to tap into the process dimension of salvation and tend to remain infantile in their ability to discern spiritual things and lead a godly life. Therefore, they are of little use to the ministry of Christ. On the other hand, those who ignore the FOR US dimension and only focus on the IN US dimension of salvation are often bound into legalistic notions of having to earn their salvation by becoming righteous or holy enough to earn it. Finally, those who only focus on the TO US dimension are often confused concerning the status of their salvation and often resign themselves to a mentality of "I guess I won't know until Jesus comes back." All three of these groups are usually miserable and tend to experience spiritual burnout rather quickly.

The more balanced position on salvation that acknowledges all four dimensions (and thus incorporates all the scriptures on salvation) suggests that by accepting what Christ has done FOR US, we are saved, and are elevated to a spiritual position of righteousness with God. Nevertheless, God is currently in the process of developing that salvation IN US so that our souls and bodies will eventually conform to the righteousness that we already obtained spiritually. We yield to this salvation IN US also recognizing the fact that God wants to export this salvation THROUGH US to redeem the rest of the world. Finally, we recognize that the salvation that is currently in progress IN US and THROUGH US will ultimately be consummated when Jesus comes again and brings completion TO US.

Just as I have applied these dimensions to understanding salvation, one could also apply them to understanding other important concepts in the Bible like righteousness, justification, holiness, and sanctification. Table 6.1 above provides some examples for each of the 4 dimensions on some crucial Bible topics.

There are at least two benefits to utilizing these dimensions when we study biblical concepts. The first is that we will achieve thoroughness and comprehensiveness in our study. In other words, we will be able to search for and discover the full range of what God has to say about a topic. Secondly, we will maintain balance in our understanding of what the Bible has to say about these topics. Hopefully, we will avoid focusing in on and building entire doctrines around just one dimension of what the Bible has to say about something.

Learning to think of the Bible and the will of God along these four dimensions will help us to more fully appreciate the diversity of the word of God in all of its glory. Moreover, it will help us to understand the will of God better so that we can take our stand and cooperate with the current and future workings of God.

My challenge for you, the reader, is to take some time when you are reading the Bible to think about how these dimensions are being used in whatever text you are reading. See if you recognize which dimension is being presented on the topic that you are reading about. Furthermore, spend some time thinking about the dimensions that are not being presented in the text. Try to see if you can find some verses that do address these other dimensions. In doing so, your study will become more comprehensive, and thus, more balanced. God Bless!